So, You Want a Gr

A must read for all nev

Book 1 in the *Essential Canine Life Skills* Series

Essex Dog Training

Acknowledgements must go to Ade Parker from Ade Parker Photography for the cover. Please visit his website at www.adeparkerphotography.com

Introduction

Hi, my name is Emma Jane, and I am the owner and head trainer at Essex Dog Training. I qualified as a dog trainer almost a decade ago and have helped hundreds of dog and human partnerships like yours achieve their goals.

There is so much information available on how to welcome your new pup into your home, what you should and should not do, everyone will have an opinion for you and of course their opinion will be the right one!

New pup ownership can be a scary time for new dog parents and with all these different opinions, many people do not know which way to turn and then lack the confidence that is needed to raise their new pup.

In turn, this will bring its own set of problems, as the one thing pup will need is confidence and harmony. As a new pup owner, trying to stay calm and having firm goals set out should be your priority.

This book is for those of you who want to use reward based, positive training methods, whilst maintaining good boundaries and sensible expectations and therefore establishing good manners for your new puppy.

It will help you achieve a good foundation for a solid, well rounded, and good-mannered relationship with your grown-up dog. Your pup will be willing to learn whatever you decide to teach him!

Training a dog takes time and patience. Set yourself goals and ensure you fully understand the exercises before carrying out with your dog.

All our books are also available as courses with trainer guidance on our website www.essexdogtraining.co.uk

Chapter One:
Giving your pup a safe place to live

Before your pup arrives, you should purchase a dog crate and place it in the space that you want your pup's 'bedroom' to be. If you want to give them an extension to this area, then you can use baby gates or puppy pens to help secure it and place your crate in to finalise your pup's bedroom.

The advantages of crate training your pup are numerous. Your pup will relish the thought of having a safe area. Journeys in the car, and vet stays will be easier for them to cope with. It will also help if your pup needs to stay with someone else or you go on holiday with unfamiliar territory. Immediately, life will be familiar for them with their safe place.

Having a crate will give them an area they can take themselves off to if they want to be alone. It will encourage independent sleep times and this in turn will help prevent separation anxiety and help you develop a confident, well-balanced sleep pattern.

Ensure your crate is placed in a good quiet place, avoiding outside walls where there may be noises from the garden that may cause disruption from foxes or small animals. Busy walkways can also be disruptive for pups.

Before your pup comes home place a blanket in the crate. This ideally should have been with your pup's litter for a couple of weeks prior to them coming home. Where possible, avoid washing this blanket for the first couple of weeks.

Crate training is very simple for young pups. If the crate provides them with all their essential needs, they will soon settle alone without you. It will provide them with safety, warmth, comfort, food, and water.

Be persistent, confident, and calm that it is a safe area for your pup. This in turn will encourage the independence and calm that your dog needs to become balanced. Of course, expect some sleepless nights and if your pup is too distressed, then pop downstairs with minimal lighting, or contact and ensure the pup is safe. It's advised that these visits are soon weaned off.

Place their only water bowl in their bedroom/crate and do not offer any other source of water for the early days. It can be removed at bedtime.

Cover three sides of the crate to create security, with something that they can't drag in and then you can have a long piece of material that you can cover the door with over-night and during their daytime sleeps.

By feeding their meals in the crate you can very simply 'train' your dog that this bedroom is a lovely place to be. Young pups may be scared when they first come home, this bedroom is a simple replica of a safe place they would find if they got lost.

Common mistakes made are thoughts that the pup doesn't like it or would prefer a different type of bedding etc. Keep it simple in the early days, remember if your pup sees you constantly changing things from day one, he or she will not be settled.

Next, check your garden for safety, poison plants, fix any holes in fences, loose stones etc. All this should be done before the new pup arrives. If you want to establish just a small area in your garden for toilet training, then this should be firmly enclosed and ideally near to the back door. Puppy pads are not needed around the house, and you will be able to train your dog to go to the toilet outside if you keep this area clean.

Remember to secure any area that you want to use properly. Once your pup has learnt to escape, they will be forever testing their boundaries! Have a good look around your home, remove anything that might be tempting for a new pup. Ensure loose cables are fixed and away. Secure loose carpets and fraying edges. Anything you have that you feel your pup may like to play with needs to be safe and secure.

Give your pup a sensory play pen area, this will give them positive experiences with different toys, different surfaces, and different games at times. All of this will help to encourage confident, independent dogs in the long term. It should not be used for hours on end, simply as a play area from time to time.

It would be helpful to sit down with your family and establish the pup's boundaries. You can use star charts for children to set them goals. They should be reminded that the pup is not a toy, but an animal, and they should be encouraged to care for and look after their new dog and be taught to interact properly.

Establish your own puppy rules. Do you want your pup to sleep on your furniture? Go upstairs? Are there other areas of the house that you do not want the pup in? Stick to them and be persistent – your pup will learn. It is not a good idea to let pups upstairs in the first few months simply because they will see it as the place we sleep in and our scents and smells are the strongest. You are quite likely to get hidden wees upstairs in these areas. This rule does not have to be for a lifetime, but it will help you in the early days.

Keep this list and ensure you stick by it – you are training your pup, not the other way round!

Chapter Two:
The early days at home

When you bring your pup home, he/she is likely to be tired and maybe feeling a little lost. This is very normal and placing your pup in their new bedroom for an hour or so will help them to settle and establish this area as a safe place for them. Resist the temptation to let the pup explore their new empire.

Take the pup outside to see if they toilet and then allow them to explore a little more. Have lots of safe toys and objects that they can chew. Be inventive: toilet roll cartons and such like make great destructive games that your pup will love, and which will keep your own property safe. Offer the pup a small feed and then they will probably be ready for another sleep in their bedroom.

Continue this routine for the first few weeks. Feed all mealtimes in their bedroom/crate area and do not allow pup to graze feed. If the meal is not eaten with 15 minutes, then pop it away and offer it at the next mealtime. Be consistent – do not offer any other food within the first few weeks, not even edible chews (you can use frozen carrots for teething time or big rope knots or chew toys to help).

If you offer your pup lots of different things to eat, they could become fussy eaters. Worse still, they can develop skin irritations or upset tums and you will have no idea which food source is causing the problem. There is plenty of time for this once they're older.

Also, by not offering them anything other than their food it will be much easier for you to toilet train your pup.

You can use their food for training. If you decide to feed raw, you can hand feed them with a spoon. This all helps bonding.

It is personal preference if you decide to feed raw products or kibble biscuits. Speak with your local stockist and go with what suits you. The only real thing to remember here is that you need to feed a high content of meat as dogs are carnivores. A good quality kibble biscuit these days has a bare minimum of 65% meat content. Avoid fillers such as grain and rice, which can cause problems for your dogs.

By establishing a routine of all meals to be fed in their crate, their daytime naps in their bedroom/crate area (shut and covered), you are teaching the pup that this area will give them all the safety and security they need.

In time this will help establish confident and balanced dogs and could help to stop the development of anxiety issues at a later stage. It is true to say that some pups are just born this way, but at least you have done everything you can to try to avoid it.

Continue with the toilet training. If your dog has an accident indoors, ignore it. Be patient – every new pup owner should expect accidents indoors. The only place that you should have a puppy pad is in their crate overnight. All other times it is recommended you take your pup outside to where you want the pup to go to the toilet. Just ensure the area is clean and safe for pup.

Try to stay quiet and just walk around while you take them outside. Move about a little to promote sniffing and movement from pup. Once they have 'performed', give them plenty of praise and remember to smile.

You could food reward, but you do not want to become a vending machine for your dog, and food is very useful for merit behaviours that we need later. Let your pup know you are happy with them and smile and praise and congratulate them for doing the right thing.

Pups should be taken outside to go to the toilet a bare minimum of every hour. You will reap the results of putting in this early work. If you follow a good toilet programme, most pups will be clean indoors within a couple of weeks. If the days are sunny and warm, be sure you still close the door to your garden. This way the pup will learn to ask you to open the door to go outside.

You will start to notice patterns from your puppy. You will recognise when the pup is tired, needs the toilet, needs something to chew or just wants to be round you.

Always watch and observe your pup. Let them discover their new surroundings. Have a boundless supply of good quality toys lying around that you want them to have. If they go for something you don't want them to have, a simple diversion of you playing with one of their toys will be enough in these early days.

Try switching toys around. By having a box available of toys they have not seen for a while will be like giving them a birthday present. It will renew their interest in their toys.

Start to establish some good manners around toys and doorways. Remember everything they want in these early days is a reward for them, even a fuss from you. If you do not want your dog to jump up or nip you, then you should not reward it or reinforce what they are doing. Freezing your body language and interaction completely is a great way of ensuring you are not reinforcing the behaviour. As soon as your pup stops nipping, carry on with what you were doing.

Ignore them, walk away but be sure to give them a fuss when next time, their four feet are on the floor.

Try to remember that by pushing your pup away you are encouraging rough play behaviour, this could be a reward for them. If they are tugging at your sleeve, arm, or trouser leg they want the tug they enjoy. If you push and pull back this will create one happy puppy with lots of adrenaline!

Stop all interaction – stop any motion, stop any sound. They will usually give up, however if your pup is a persistent offender then some pups will respond if you make the noise of a hurt pup, still ensure very little interaction, just squeal, be still and carry on once they have stopped. If your pup is consistently nipping you, then it is ready for some mind games and some brain training. If at any time you feel overwhelmed or are struggling, you need to enlist the help of a qualified trainer.

It is up to you if you reward your pup for four feet on the floor or a sit or a mixture of both. But do establish that if there's anything they want, you will wait for this behaviour – if they jump and snatch, it is not good manners, wait patiently for their please and then release them with their toy.

Give the behaviour you want a cue/word, e.g. "floor" or "sit" would work well. Praise the behaviour and give them what they want. Even going forward out of a door is a reward. It is all good manners training for them. Do not be a dictator, and ask with a calm voice.

In the early weeks of arrival your pup will not receive many 'formal' training sessions, and the training will all be around good manners. This is by far the most important part of establishing a well-mannered, balanced pet.

Ensuring your pup has play times in its pen area and sleep times in their crate will also give your children a chance to run around and drop as many toys as they want so they can maintain 'their time' too.

Encourage healthy relationships between dogs and children by showing them how to play with their dog – not treating the pup as their toy. They should play with the puppy with the pup's toy. A simple game of fetch can be taught by throwing a toy and sitting patiently until the pup brings it to you and then rewarding them with lots of praise and a game and a re-throw out.

Ensure the children do not steal the pups' toys and vice versa. Do not leave young children with the pup unsupervised. Have strict guidelines for both the pup and your children. Using sticker charts is a great way to get your children engaged.

Do not allow the children to go into the pup's crate and do not allow the pup to go into their bedrooms.

If you are at home for long periods of time, be sure that your pup is given time away from you. Do not allow your pup to develop 'FOMO – fear of missing out!' It is quite close to separation anxiety, but allowing your pup to have time alone will really help him/her to establish more confidence and independence. Try to get a healthy balance of time with you and time alone. If you also allow too much time alone, then separation anxiety could manifest. If you manage to get the perfect balance, then you will reap the rewards.

Chapter Three:
Socialisation

You should start to take your pup out to lots of different places and get them experienced with different noises, sounds and experiences. Try to keep life very normal and relaxed. This will create great socialisation and is different to socialising with other dogs.

Your dog just needs to be comfortable in their surroundings. Rush them and they could become fearful, so be sure to move at your dogs' pace. This is best done pre-vaccination so be inventive. Baby slings can be useful for small pups – prams or such like for bigger ones.

Do get them out to everywhere you think they may visit throughout their lives. If you are a family who like to eat out and want to be able to take them to your favourite café, then take them out as a pup. Let them experience different noises, different surfaces, and see lots of different things. Plan days out so they can see these things. If you take your pup to the vets every week to use their scales and get the reception staff to pop them a treat, they will soon realise the vets is a good place to be.

Do not make an issue out of going out and be as relaxed as you can. Sitting on your lap watching your children play football in the park is a great way of socialising with lots of different noises etc.

Laughing and joking with friends by a busy road while your pup is in your arms is a great way of socialising them with traffic. Do not allow people to come and poke your puppy. This is not good socialisation and will often make pups fearful of people.

Regular short fun trips in the car (crated) are a good idea, as is using public transport if this is the norm for your life.

Do not over-expose your dog – just a calm walk on different days of the week at different times will generally be good socialisation for your puppy. (Ensure you keep a diary – you will surprise yourself with how many different things you have successful exposed your pup to).

Resist the urge to take them up to every single person or dog they meet. Just walk along by and they will soon be relaxed in their surroundings. They need to know that the most important person when they are out is you — this will encourage amazing recall. So, reward them a lot with small treats or their dinner while you are out, and it will encourage them to be balanced and want to be with you. If you can, work with people you trust, then ensure your pup gets interaction with people too. People that are interacting with your pup should be kind and thoughtful and move at your pups' pace.

Pick your dog's friends carefully. Enlist the help of some of your own friends and join some dog walking friends if you can. Busy day-care centres and dog parks are not good places for puppies. It can make them reactive on the lead and they could end up being bullied, too. Your pup needs to play with nice dogs and owners that you know are canine responsible.

Ensure that you do not put your pup into danger by approaching unknown dogs. Not all dogs like puppies and a swift bite from an older dog is not unheard of. It could make your pup anxious around other dogs. Read your pup's body language and be confident with your decision. If your pup does not look happy, then remove them from the situation. Rough and tumble play, however, is very normal and if your pup finds a kind buddy, then regular play meet ups can be amazing.

How much pup plays with other dogs you encourage is dependent on what you want from your dog. For instance, a person that wants to work their dog in agility or other sports will be working on more focus on them around other dogs, this pup will grow up wanting more interaction with their owners than other dogs, and vice versa. Try to find the right balance for you and your family.

A sporting dog is less likely to grow up wanting to play in a group. If you are just looking for a balanced pup trained enough focus on you to gain good recall but meet up with friends too, be slightly cautious in the early days – if you let some working breed dogs off lead too early without lots of interaction with you, the pup will soon learn that running off searching for scents or playmates is much more rewarding than being with you!

Reading your pup's emotions is the key to getting a good balance of confidence and focus on you, whilst you are giving them a great experience of all the sights and sounds they need to see.
If you want your pup to be totally focused on you, take a meal out with them and hand feed and smile at your pup.

Chapter Four:
Formal Training

Your pup will only need a few minutes of formal training a couple of times each day to establish a good response to their name, a relationship with you and a sit and wait until given permission. You can hand feed one or two of their meals for these sessions.

The remainder of the time your pup is in discovery mode. It is so important to establish your boundaries and expectations from the very first day your puppy arrives. By using the reward methods in the previous section of this book, you will keep establishing good manners and boundaries. Never give up and make sure you always smile and praise good behaviour.

Remember, your new pup is like a sponge in the early days. They have not brought a book to learn how to get your attention or to learn how to read you. They are doing it from day one and can be amazingly good at it.

Confidence and being realistic and fair in what you want to achieve is all you need for a good start to achieving your well-mannered pet dog.

Some pups do not particularly like being stroked at certain times – particularly if over aroused. Do try to stoke during training times but if your pup does not like being stroked while you train then it is not rewarding for them, smile and praise instead.

The formal training you will need in the early days is very simple. You are looking to concentrate on good manners and proving yourself to be a fun teacher for your dog. It is suggested that you mix the following list into different sessions that are short and very fun. In the early days food is a great reinforcer but do ensure that you always praise, smile, and have fun with your dog. This will ensure that your dogs' relationship is with you, not just the piece of food.

Good Name Response

Have the dog's bowl of food with you, take out a biscuit or a spoonful of their raw food and call their name in an inviting way, and when they come to you smile praise and food reward.

Make sure you are not over-using the dog's name during the day. It should mean 'come to me, I have something good for you'
Use it only when you have something good for your pup and when you smile at them.

If they are doing something you do not want them to do, try using the words "leave" or "drop" instead. If a pup does not like giving these things up, developing a 'swap' with food in the early days is a very useful tool and you can use food for this.

You can teach them to have a good name response at various times during the day – just call them when you have something good for them and don't use it at other times or to steer them around the house.

Teaching your pup to take a treat or toy gently

Hold a piece of their kibble slightly in front of their nose. If they try to grab or snatch at the food, do not reprimand or mark this behaviour in any way. Silently close your hand withholding the reward. Remember your dog is trying to work out what gets him his reward or attention. Let their brain work and be a patient, calm, and kind teacher.

The instant they are quiet with their feet on the floor, mark the behaviour with a quick "yes" and open your hand to reward instantly. Some pups you will need to be more patient than others with, but patience is the key. No interaction from you until you succeed will get much quicker success.

Ensuring pup does not jump up

Once you have established good manners with food, then you can start to ensure that your pup is polite for everything they want in their life. Make sure that everything you offer your pup, they settle on the floor and do not jump and grab. Mark the settling behaviour with a quick "yes" or "good" and then give them the toy/bone. Ensuring your delivery of the reward is low will help to encourage your pup.

If they jump, do not snatch it away, just wait for the settle – they could find snatching and jumping fun!

Repeat the same exercise with a smile as the reward and soon they will get the idea if they settle, they will get what they want. If they jump and snatch, no interaction is rewarded.

Try not to push or use your hands as the pup will often see this as a game. Over excited behaviour by you or family members/visitors will encourage jumping up – so be sure to be strict with everyone who deals with the pup to be calm and ignore on initial contact.

Also, if they are jumping up at the door of the crate, just simply wait for their feet to be on the floor and then open the gate. You are simply saying to them (with your actions) that if you give me bad manners, you do not get what you want – if you have good manners, then you do.

This will help to ensure that your dog is well mannered. It is much easier to train obedience if you have a well-mannered dog.

Teaching your pup a sit and mini wait

A sit and mini wait can start to be taught once you have taught your dog the good manners above. There is no set time for this, just progress your pup at their own pace.

Start the sit by gently pushing the treat backwards over your pup's head and then when they are in position say the words, "good sit".

Do not use the command/cue 'sit' to gain the position until the dog is offering on its own. You are speaking a foreign language to your pup – use it kindly and in a rewarding way.

Reinforce the sit in lots of different ways and any time your dog sits during the day praise should be given. You will find your dog starts to offer you a sit at various times – just praise and say "good sit" every time they do.

Encourage focus on you in the sit by smiling at your dog and being happy when you see them – try this in lots of different places.

Ending your training session

You can either hand feed the whole meal or just a little and then place the dish back in their bed where they can finish the meal in peace. Saying the words "in your bed" as you place the bowl will train the word 'bed'. If you are training and it is not a mealtime, you can add a "finish" cue to the end of your session and toss a treat to the side. Be sure your body language says no further interaction with me. By giving your pup something to chew independently will help to increase politeness and stop pup chewing at your legs and trousers for more interaction.

After the first few days make sure the pup goes in the crate first before you put the bowl in (this will stop negotiating behaviour later when we do more formal training).

Always keep some of one of their other meals back and have it on you in your pocket (obviously use treats if you feed raw). This way you can reward name calling at different times of the day and in different situations. Do not use their name more than a few times a day and ONLY when you want them to come to you for something good!

These early weeks just use lots of praise and sometimes their biscuits – do not use high value treats yet. Save them for outdoor work.

Expected behaviour at kerbs etc. should be a sit, reinforce with praise and smiles – your dog will love to make you smile. The mini wait can also be used and as you walk forward say "okay" as a release of behaviour.

Chapter Five
Moving Forward

Your short, happy, formal training should now be done daily in lots of different places, stick with the sit and mini wait (just as part of your daily regime going through doors etc. – remember moving off and forward is the reinforcer/reward for your dog), keep everything light hearted, fun and full of lots and praise.

At the moment, try not to use your top treats (except if you are in class where kibble may not be enough!). If your dog enjoys their lead being put on, then this is a reward. Make sure they sit when you put it on, praise and smile.

Explore what your dog likes – if they like playing with a toy then use this for training, too, and have lots of fun with them.

This early routine will really help to build a healthy relationship and bond with your dog. Always smile when your pup looks at you and be happy to see them!

Confident handling of new pups is essential, and inspection of paws, claws, teeth etc. should be routine.

Owners should look for bright clean eyes, pink lips and healthy gums, as well as doing regular coat inspections for ticks, and grooming of long-haired dogs.

Do not cause pain to your pup whilst handling them – be confident and calm. A small treat and fuss after inspection will teach them that being handled is a good thing. Your groomer and vet will thank you for this.

When the time comes to reprimand your pup, and it will, then use a quick effective change of voice tone and body language. Almost like a kind headmaster. Ensure you're confident in your behaviour so it is effective, and the pup is in no doubt that it did the wrong thing. If you have taught all the above manners, your pup will be quick to respond. The use of physical punishment, time out etc. is not needed or required. Do not use the dog's name at this time, simply tell your dog what you want him/her to do – "leave" "drop" or "come" away are good instructions.

For persistent offenders you will need to look at what is triggering your pup's behaviour. They may be ready for some more brain work. Perhaps your pup is ready to graduate onto our basic training book. Do not leave it to see if it will sort itself out – it will not.

If you see something wrong about to happen, get good at diverting pup with something you want them to have, such as a toy/bone etc. Get the balance between a good diversion, and enough is enough. Do not hold a grudge with your pup. Move on from the situation quickly and with praise for the right behaviour. Pups do not do well around stress, emotion, or grudges.

Summary

The most important things for you and your pup are confidence and boundaries. Make sure you are having lots of fun with your pup. Training should never be about dictatorship.

Have a think about what sort of dog you want to end up with. If you want your dog to become totally focused on you so that you can train to do some of the popular dog sports, such as agility and tricks, then you need to work on focus on you in as many different places as possible.

If you want your dog to become a well-behaved balanced pet, and enjoying family walks with friends and other dogs is important to you, then choose some dog friends and meet up regularly then you could do less focus work but enough to have a good response under distraction.

Whatever you decide, your pup will now be ready for some more formal training. He or she could be showing signs of boredom and all dogs benefit from continued training.

Attending classes these days isn't necessary – in fact some dogs do not do well in a class situation. There are lots of options available to the pup owner and the next step is personal preference.

By following this simple to read pup book you have started your pup on an amazing journey, you should be proud of yourself for giving your pup the very best start you possibly can.

Be sure to reward yourself. Pup training is hard! You and your pup will start to have an incredible bond and where the future lies is in your hands. Enjoy it together.

Further Training

Also available in the Essential Canine Life Skills series:

So, You Want a Great Puppy
So, You Want Amazing Basic Training
So, You Want Incredible Dog Recall
So, You Want Fantastic Loose Lead Walking
So, You Want to Reduce Your Dog's Barking

Want personalised help from Emma and her team?

Essex Dog training offers customised dog training packages, and one-to-one instruction to clients all around the world. Visit www.essexdogtraining.co.uk to find out how we can help you train the dog of your dreams.

About the Author

Emma Jane is a qualified dog trainer with many years of experience helping hundreds of dog-owner partnerships achieve their potential. In 2013 she took her passion to a new level, founding Essex Dog Training to share her ethos of building harmonious partnerships through compassion and understanding.

Prior to that she worked with local authorities as an alternative education provider, and many of the skills she learned there continue to benefit the people and dogs she teaches.

Emma has always had a strong connection with dogs, and she has competed with her dogs at the international dog show Crufts, earning her place on the podium, which she credits to the incredible bond they share.

To learn more about Emma's methods and philosophy, visit her website: www.essexdogtraining.co.uk

Printed in Great Britain
by Amazon